C000066288

1

Pocketbook

By Bruce Potts

Cartoons:
Phil Hailstone

Published by:

Teachers' Pocketbooks
Laurel House, Station Approach,
Alresford, Hampshire SO24 9JH, UK
Tel: +44 (0)1962 735573
Fax: +44 (0)1962 733637
E-mail: sales@teacherspocketbooks.co.uk
Website: www.teacherspocketbooks.co.uk

*Teachers' Pocketbooks is an imprint of
Management Pocketbooks Ltd.*

Series Consultant: **Brin Best**.

This edition published 2004.

ISBN 1 90377661 9

British Library Cataloguing-in-Publication
Data – A catalogue record for this book is
available from the British Library.

Design, typesetting and graphics by Efex Ltd.
Printed in UK.

Contents

Primary school should be
a magical experience,
and in many schools it is.
It should amaze and
inspire and thrill.

Charles Clarke

How to use this pocketbook

This pocketbook is aimed at teachers working with primary children and is intended to provide a wealth of practical tips, ideas and suggestions to help you be an even better teacher than you already are. It is laid out so that you can quickly find ideas to use in the classroom, and it unashamedly focuses on your main (and most important) role: teaching your children. You may have other responsibilities within the school but this book doesn't try to deal with that.

The ideas and suggestions here have been put together from my own experiences as a teacher over 25 years, as well as the combined experiences of the many wonderfully creative, caring and dedicated teachers I have both worked with and observed in schools around the country during that time.

At the end of each section is a short self-evaluation checklist for you to identify your own strengths and possible areas for development.

How to use this pocketbook

The content of this book arises from our growing understanding of:

1. How children learn most effectively.
2. How *and why* children don't succeed.
3. The forms of classroom organisation and management that support effective teaching and learning, and the repertoire that serves these ends.
4. The principles that underpin teachers' work, ie:
   - Children learn most effectively when they feel emotionally secure
   - High quality achievement depends upon structured progression based upon continuity of curriculum experience
   - High quality pupil achievement arises directly from a consistent set of high expectations
   - Teaching should be fun for the teacher and learning should be fun for the learner

The Role of the
Primary Teacher

 Classroom
Organisation

 Creating the
Emotionally Supportive
Learning Environment

 Being the
'Great Teacher'

 Relationships

 Looking After
Yourself

 Successful OFSTED
Inspections

The Role of the Primary Teacher

Background to primary teaching

In 1967 the Plowden Report was published. It set out clearly what primary education was about, stating: *'At the heart of the educational process lies the child'*. Many schools adopted this notion as the central plank of their educational philosophy, but very few schools created an organised structure within which such a philosophy could flourish. Consequently, many teachers were left to deliver whatever they thought was appropriate for their children without having to consider the wider picture across their own school, let alone across the country. Whilst this led to inspirational and exciting teaching and learning activities in many schools, it did not guarantee any kind of continuity and progression for children. There was no certainty anywhere in the country about what children could expect to have learned by the time they left their primary schools.

The introduction of the National Curriculum in the late 1980s was an attempt to address this lack of cohesion in primary education nationally and to guarantee a certain level of provision in terms of knowledge, skills and understanding for all our children. And so began the period when education found itself at the heart of political argument and at last began to get the kind of attention it had never received before.

Background to primary teaching

Unfortunately, along with political interest came political direction. Successive administrations took increasing control of the content and structure of the primary curriculum, establishing the notion that not only **what** is taught but also **how** it is taught should be determined by Government. As a result, there emerged a number of different initiatives for teachers to adopt, not least the Literacy and Numeracy Strategies. These set out clearly and unequivocally what and how English and Maths should be taught. Along with these initiatives have come a range of other strategies. Some, such as Local Management of Schools, were intended to give schools greater local flexibility; others (eg: OFSTED, Performance Management, Target Setting, National Curriculum Tests in Year 2 and Year 6 and the publication of league tables) ostensibly held the desired aim of 'raising standards' – whatever that means.

Whilst many of these changes were undoubtedly needed to ensure some kind of national unity of purpose within primary education, there is the feeling that we may have lost sight of the true meaning of primary education. Many teachers have almost forgotten what they originally came into primary teaching for, so distracted are they by having to 'deliver' the latest expected outcome for the government, the LEA or some other stakeholder.

Children come to
school to play and to
see their friends
(we think they come to
school to learn!)

Background to primary teaching

Children don't choose to come to school; parents just send them when they reach the appropriate age.

When my son Elliott first started school in the reception class I remember him coming home after his first day and when I asked what he had done at school he replied, '*Nothing*'. This went on for the first three days, which led me to change the question to, '*Who did you play with at school today?*' At this point he launched into a long explanation about everything that had happened at school that day, starting with what he had done at playtime and lunchtime. Even now, though he is sixteen, I still start each evening by asking him about his friends and what he did at break rather than talking about work!

I realised then, if I hadn't already realised before, that in the mind of a child, school is there for play and for friendships. So, not only does playtime itself have to be a rewarding and fun experience, the whole learning experience has to feel like play and we all have to be their friends. It is only when young children feel the sense of belonging that comes through friendship, and the sense of fun and fulfilment that comes through play, that they are truly happy and will learn effectively.

Background to primary teaching

As I travel around the country in my role as educational consultant and trainer, I am reassured by some outstanding examples of inspirational teaching and learning that the philosophy of primary education which places children at the heart of the process is still alive and well in many schools.

My aim in writing this book is to bring to you some of the principles which underpin that philosophy. The hope is that we can combine the rich diet of creativity, inspiration and spontaneity that used to exist with the rigour, organisation and certainty introduced since 1988 to create schools in which high-achieving children work in exciting classrooms with inspirational and dynamic teachers. Because primary teaching is the best job in the world.

> **Learning should be fun – let's make it so.**

Roles and responsibilities

Formally, teachers' roles and responsibilities are clearly set out in the Teachers' Pay and Conditions document which is updated each year. But let's put aside the boring bit for the moment while we consider what your role *really* involves. To my mind the role of the primary teacher is to:

- Lead by example and try to be an exemplary role model for children to follow
- Inspire and motivate children to believe they can do anything – ignite the spark
- Take children on a 'Learning Adventure' every day
- Lead children to where they've never been before – you're the Pied Piper and they'll go anywhere you want to take them!
- Excite and stimulate children's natural curiosity, imagination and creativity
- Raise self-esteem and self-belief, and by so doing create thinking, self-motivated and high-achieving learners
- Prepare children for the society in which they are going to live and work
- Send them on to secondary school with all the skills, attitudes, knowledge and resilience they need to succeed

And don't forget – you are one of the most influential people in a young child's life, in some cases **the** most influential. You can change their life!

Roles and responsibilities

So now we understand what your roles and responsibilities really are, how does that manifest itself in the perception of the young learner in your classroom? If you have adopted the above principles in the way that you operate, and combine them with some of the suggestions contained later in this book about creating an emotionally supportive environment and delivering inspirational learning, your children will soon be:

- Leaping out of bed in the morning to get ready for school because they're about to spend *another* amazing day in your classroom
- Enjoying every moment of the day
- Happy, fulfilled and motivated learners
- Caring, thoughtful and helpful children
- Sad at home time because it means the school day is over

Policies and procedures

As a teacher you will have your own ideas about how you like to do things. In many cases that's fine, but you will need to be fully aware of the stated expectations of the school as laid out in the various policy statements which undoubtedly exist. It is your responsibility to ensure that you are following the agreed policies. It is not easy to keep fully up to date with every single expectation in every single policy statement; however, there are some policies with which you really must become fully familiar, preferably before you start working in the school (so request them after you have been appointed but before you take up your post) or at the latest in your first week in your new job.

Teaching and learning
This policy should set out precisely what the expectations are within the school for teaching and learning. There may also be statements about the learning environment and certain expectations for planning and presentation of children's work. You should become thoroughly familiar with this policy, so take time to sit down and go through it in detail. It is, after all, probably the most important policy in the school.

Policies and procedures

Behaviour

Children's conduct is most effectively managed in schools where there is an agreed set of rewards and sanctions and the expectations for behaviour are clearly understood by children and adults alike. Consequently, it's important that you follow the school's agreed behaviour policy, even though you may supplement it with some of your own ideas within your classroom. Again, become fully familiar with this policy.

Child protection

Children arrive at school every day with all kinds of emotional (and sometimes physical) baggage which in some cases hinders their learning prospects and in other cases may be harming them. Although it is not your personal responsibility to deal with child protection, the school's child protection procedures will be clearly outlined in this policy and will guide you in what you should do should you have any concern at all about a child. Spend time becoming familiar with these procedures and make sure you know who the designated 'lead professional' is for any of your children who are 'at risk'.

Policies and procedures

Health and safety
Read this policy! It will state clearly those aspects of health and safety which directly impact on your job – you **must** understand the implications.

Other policies
There will of course be many other policies in your school which you can become more familiar with over time. Try to ensure that you have read them *all* as soon as is practicably possible and definitely by the end of your first year in the school.

Other procedures
Some of the many procedures and systems will appear alien to you when you first start in a school. Don't worry – you'll soon get the hang of them. Don't be afraid to ask if you're not sure of something.

Your place within the school

Hierarchies exist within any organisation and this is no different in a primary school, so where do you fit in? There's no more important job in a primary school than class teacher, so don't let anyone tell you any different, even though there are many people doing many other jobs alongside you. You will have a variety of responsibilities to colleagues, parents and others but your most important responsibility is to your children. As a rule of thumb try to:

- Follow all agreed school policies
- Arrive for meetings on time
- Arrive early each day for school
- Work *with* rather than against colleagues
- Avoid seeing parents at the start of the school day if at all possible
- Spend time in the staff room – it is important to spend time with colleagues to share successes (and failures!) and to build positive relationships
- Attend as many of the PTA events as you feel able to – and join in
- Be friendly with support staff and treat them with respect
- Be ready to teach five minutes before children arrive

Expectations of self

Do you have high expectations of yourself? Of course you do, but what exactly do we mean by this? The best teachers I've seen have certain common characteristics. They:

- Love being with children (seems obvious doesn't it, but it's not always the case)
- Constantly strive to improve their teaching, always looking for new ideas to enhance their practice
- Aren't afraid to ask others who they perceive have a better way of doing something
- Model the behaviours they expect of their students
- Are on a learning journey themselves
- Are energetic and enthusiastic
- Always have time for children
- Do things differently
- Create positive energy around them
- Are innovative and prepared to take risks
- Are friendly and approachable

Do you have some (or all) of the above characteristics? Read each statement in turn and identify what you think you might need to do to develop these characteristics.

A self-evaluation checklist

	A	B	C
I lead by example and try to be a good role model for my children			
I am fully conversant with the school's Teaching and Learning Policy			
Child protection procedures are fully understood			
My classroom is healthy and safe			
I follow the agreed school policies and procedures			
I regularly find time to be with my colleagues in the staffroom			
I attend PTA functions			
When children arrive in the classroom I am ready for them			
I get along with my colleagues			
I love the company of my children			
I'm energetic and enthusiastic			
Children find me approachable and friendly			
I'm creative and innovative in my teaching			
I arrive on time for meetings			

A – strength   **B – not sure**   **C – area for development**

The Role of the
Primary Teacher

 Classroom
Organisation ◀

 Creating the
Emotionally Supportive
Learning Environment

 Being the
'Great Teacher'

 Relationships

 Looking After
Yourself

 Successful OFSTED
Inspections

Classroom Organisation

Furniture

Your classroom is your second home for the year and as such you need to ensure that you have all the furniture you need to do your job effectively and efficiently. Before the autumn term starts ensure that you have adequate furniture for yourself *and* for your children.

For yourself
- Enough storage space for files and folders, etc
- A desk (if you use one) and chair for your use
- Any other furniture you think you may need

For the children:
- A desk and chair appropriate to their age and size
- Storage furniture so that all materials and resources can be tidily and accessibly stored leaving surfaces free of unnecessary clutter

Furniture

Be prepared to reorganise the furniture to accommodate different learning situations.

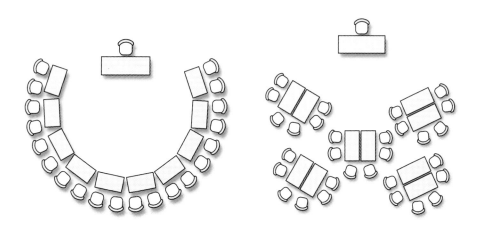

Materials and resources

In the well-organised classroom all materials and resources are properly organised so that everything is easily accessible for children's use. Go through this checklist to see how your classroom matches up.

Materials and resources are stored neatly and tidily	
All storage containers are easily accessible	
All materials and resources are clearly labelled	
Children know where everything can be found	
There is no unnecessary clutter on flat surfaces	
The classroom is a well-ordered learning environment	

So – is yours the well-organised classroom? If not, what do you think you need to do to make it so?

Display

One thing that can be guaranteed to be well done in primary schools is classroom display. But what's the point of display? Is it …

- For attractiveness?
- To create interest?
- To stimulate curiosity?
- To celebrate achievement?
- For information?

However you use display make sure it:
- Is of high quality
- Reflects the agreed school display protocols
- Isn't excessive and confusing

Try using classroom display for memory mapping (see page 80) as a tool to help children remember more of what they learn.

Procedures and routines

In spite of what many people think, children respond very well to the rigour of set routines and agreed procedures. So try to establish systems for things such as:

- Lining up and entering the classroom
- What to do if the teacher is late
- Tidying up at the end of sessions
- Hanging up coats and bags
- Settling down at the beginning of lessons, ie good sitting, good listening
- Changing for PE
- Using the class resources and materials
- Carrying furniture
- Moving from class to other parts of the school

The list is endless, but once established these routines are not negotiable – stick to them!

Jobs for the boys (and jobs for the girls)

Don't children just love doing jobs for you?
(Well, most children.) One of your best
resources is the children themselves, so
use their natural willingness to help
by assigning them responsibilities
on a weekly, half-termly or termly
basis so that every child has an
important job to do. Display the
'Jobs' list for all to see.

A self-evaluation checklist

	A	B	C
Materials and resources are well organised and accessible			
There is adequate furniture for my needs			
Children's furniture is appropriate and adequate for their needs			
The classroom is uncluttered			
I reorganise the furniture to accommodate different learning situations			
Display is attractive and well used for a variety of different purposes			
We have good class systems and procedures			
A rota of jobs ensures that all children have regular class responsibilities			

A – strength   **B – not sure**   **C – area for development**

The Role of the
Primary Teacher

 Classroom
Organisation

 Creating the
Emotionally Supportive
Learning Environment ◀

 Being the
'Great Teacher'

 Relationships

 Looking After
Yourself

 Successful OFSTED
Inspections

Creating the Emotionally Supportive Learning Environment

The child's perception of you

> 'The fragrance always remains in the hand that gives the rose.'

Think back to when you were at school. Can you remember who your favourite ever teacher was? What were the characteristics that made him/her so good?

In virtually every piece of research I've come across, as well as my own research and personal experience, it is apparent that what children most want from you as their teacher is **for you to like them and care about them as individuals**. Other characteristics of effective teachers are that they:

- Are kind and caring
- Are friendly and approachable
- Don't embarrass or humiliate
- Don't have favourites
- Have a sense of humour

- Help children believe in themselves
- Are enthusiastic and energetic
- Are passionate about their subject
- Use positive, supportive language
- Make learning fun

The child's perception of you

I don't recall seeing any research into teacher effectiveness in which a child said anything along the lines of, *'She gives us great worksheets'* or, *'He marks our books so nicely'*.

Children tend to feel that if you like them then they like you, and it is this that motivates them to work hard, behave well and do their best. They begin to form a perception of you from the moment they first come into your class in September and once formed it is very difficult for you to change it. You need to create in the mind of every individual child in your class the perception that you care about them as an individual from the very beginning. This is easy to do with the child who is hard working, kind and considerate and who does everything you ask, but much more difficult to achieve with the child who constantly gives you grief or who doesn't function well in the class.

Paradoxically, it is often the most difficult children who need your positive support more than anyone else – they probably don't get it from anywhere else.

The child's perception of you

Before you can even think about teaching your children you will have to put a lot of time and effort into creating the right emotional conditions in which they can learn. Creating the right emotional environment begins with you and the atmosphere you create both around you and in your classroom.

Children learn much better when they are happy. Creating a classroom environment in which children feel a real sense of belonging and self-worth will help to raise their self-esteem and increase their motivation.

Children are amazingly adept at picking up the verbal and non-verbal signals you emit throughout your daily contact with them. Your tone of voice and body language say much more about how you feel about your children than the words you use – and they know it!

So what can we do to create an environment in which children feel liked and cared for? Read on for some ideas to try.

21 great ideas

1. Hi folks!

Where are you when children are entering your classroom at the start of sessions? Are you still faffing around at the photocopier or finishing your cup of coffee in the staff room? Try to be in the classroom **before** the children arrive so that you can greet them individually with a smile when they enter. Naturally you don't have time for a long chat, just say hello and acknowledge them all. This really helps to make them feel welcome and sets the scene for the lesson to follow.

2. 'Ere whatsisname

When you remember my name I feel important – it tells me that you care about me and that I'm not just another nameless individual in the school. Think about how often you actually use children's names when speaking to them. Try to avoid statements like, *'You three, could you tidy up the reading corner please?'* Instead say, *'Gemma, Anil and Tariq could you please tidy up the reading corner for me?'* Apply this principle when speaking to adults in the school as well – especially parents.

21 great ideas

3. No favourites – equal attention for all

It's easy to give attention to the hard-working, well-behaved child, and unfortunately the naughty child also often gets an unfair amount of your attention. Children quickly notice who is getting all the attention in the classroom and soon decide who your 'favourites' are. You need to work hard at giving equal (positive) attention to all your children so that *every* child thinks they're your favourite, even though **you** know that you don't have one. (Hard, I know, when some children are just so wonderful!) If you're not sure whether you're equally attentive to all the children, try asking a trusted colleague to observe you at work and see what they think.

4. All for one and one for all!

You and your class are likely to be together for a whole year, so it's worthwhile creating an atmosphere in which major successes are celebrated collectively. When one child (or one group of children) does something that is worthy of note, stop what everyone is doing (at an appropriate moment) and celebrate the achievement. This may be in the form of a round of applause, special certificate or even the use of music.

21 great ideas

Example: Jack and his group have worked hard for the last three weeks designing and building their Tudor house. They've put a lot of effort into it, co-operating and working as a team. They've paid particular attention to quality and have created an excellent house. Stop the class and, as the group come out to the front with their Tudor house, play the introduction to 'We are the Champions' by Queen. At the chorus, turn up the volume and give them a round of applause.

This has two effects:

- the children in the successful group feel very proud of themselves
- the rest of the children in the class want to be included, so you can use it to motivate them in the future

You can extend the celebration by giving each child in the group a 'Champion Group' sticker for their sweatshirt.

21 great ideas

5. Listen empathetically

Your children spend more time with you than anyone outside their immediate family and it is often you to whom they'll come to share a problem. Always find time to listen to them (if not now then later), not necessarily to solve the problem but mostly to be a 'friendly ear'. This is especially true when it comes to friendship problems. Don't make the mistake of trying to solve a friendship problem: with groups of girls, by the time you've found out what the problem is they've usually made up anyway; boys just tend to thump each other, shake hands and carry on as before.

6. Sing!

In all my years of experience I can hardly recall a child who didn't enjoy singing. Try to find time to sing with your children *every* day, while tidying up, waiting for everyone to arrive on the carpet, lining up for lunch, a spare two minutes after assembly. It doesn't have to be a formal music lesson, and you don't have to be a music specialist. Research what great children's songs you have in your school and start putting together your own personal repertoire. Songs with humour and/or actions work especially well.

21 great ideas

7. Aye aye captain
Children just love it when you have your own quirky ways of doing things that mark you out as different from other teachers in the school. I once worked with a teacher who insisted that the children had to respond to him with, *'Aye aye Captain'* whenever their automatic response would have been, *'Yes Mr Smith'*. Develop your own classroom rituals that help create a sense of class identity.

8. Shout it from the rooftops
It's easy to notice when children aren't doing what they should be doing and to point it out. Unfortunately this sometimes gives other children ideas they wouldn't have had before, so try to turn this around by praising them *every time* you notice them doing what you *are* looking for. Reinforce and celebrate all their positive behaviours and achievements.

9. No put-downs
Place a sign on your classroom door which simply says: *'You are now entering a No Put-Down Zone'* and then make sure everyone (including you) honours it.

21 great ideas

10. I'm in the mood

Not only do children enjoy singing, they also enjoy it when music is used in the classroom for a variety of other purposes which enhance the learning experience. Try some of these:

To...	Try...
Create class mood at the start of the day	Anything from 'Pure Classical Chillout'
Calm children as they enter class after lunch/playtime	'Meditation from Thais' by Massenet
Energise	'Tequila' by The Champs
Delineate time – tidying up	'Following the Leader' from Peter Pan or 'Colonel Hathie's March' from Jungle Book, by Disney
Delineate time – changing for PE	'Help' (Beatles, 2mins 20secs, Yr 5/6); 'Yackety Axe' (Knopfler/Atkins 3mins 20secs, Yr 3/4); 'Billy Jean' (Jackson, 4mins 55secs, KS 1)
Relax	'So Soft, Your Goodbye' by Mark Knopfler/Chet Atkins
Reinforce a message	'We're In This Together' by Simply Red or 'Proud' by Heather Small
Pure enjoyment	'Wanna be Like You' from The Jungle Book, by Disney

Research how music can enhance learning; experiment with different styles and cultures to determine when and how you use music in your classroom.

21 great ideas

11. Speaking personally…
Children love to know that you take a personal interest in them and that you notice things about their interests and lives outside of school. Try to make a mental note when Alex tells you he can't wait till Sunday because he's going to London to see his grandma. It's obviously important to him, so next time you see him make a point of asking him about it. Do this for all your children as often as you can.

12. Fair's fair
Nothing upsets children more than when they think you haven't been fair. Try to be fair and consistent in all your dealings with children and try especially hard not to react emotionally when there's a problem. Always give both sides the opportunity to give their side of the story and don't prejudge the situation just because this is a child who in the past may have caused you problems. Apply all your agreed class rules fairly and consistently and **NEVER** penalise the whole class for the misdemeanours of an individual or group.

21 great ideas

13. All say 'CHEESE'
Children are such vain creatures, don't you think? They love to talk about themselves but they also love looking at themselves, or at pictures of themselves. Create a photo display area in which every child is allowed to display a picture of themselves, perhaps with their brother, sister, mum, dad, pet, or whatever. It creates a real focal point in the class and helps to create a sense of belonging.

14. Make my day
Remember, children need to feel that you care about them, so show it by paying them compliments, not necessarily related to their work. If you happen to notice Daniel has had his hair cut in an unusual style, make a point of commenting positively on it – make him feel special. If you saw Emma riding her bike to school and using proper signals whilst doing so, tell her how impressed you were. Try to do this for every child every week, but don't leave anyone out!

21 great ideas

15. Hands up for kindness

Perhaps you have inherited a class who are really not very kind to each other and you want to change this. Keep a box full of cut-out hand shapes (out of sugar paper of course!) in an easily accessible box. Tell the children you want to try to create a circle of kindness in the class. Every time any child does something kind they collect a 'hand' from the box, write on it what their kindness was and you then Blu-Tack it to the wall above your display boards. As each successive hand goes up you will soon create a circle around the classroom. Give the children a target, say by half-term or Christmas, by which time you'd like the circle to be completed. This system can also be used for 'caring', 'thoughtfulness', 'helpfulness' or whatever you want and because it's so visual it acts as a constant reminder to all the children of what it is you are trying to achieve.

21 great ideas

16. Fantasy island

Young children still believe in Santa Claus and the Tooth Fairy and they're at an age when their lives are filled with fantasy, (which we never really grow out of if we're honest; hence the success of stories like 'Lord of the Rings' and 'Harry Potter'). Take advantage of this by playing along with them occasionally. Perhaps when you've been delayed for lessons tell them how it wasn't your fault because you were abducted by aliens! Or tell them about the time when you really went through the wardrobe into the land of Narnia and what you found there.

17. It's all a mystery to me!

Similarly, use objects such as feely bags, feely boxes or a 'mystery suitcase' as part of your normal repertoire of activities in the classroom to create a sense of expectancy and mystery for the children.

21 great ideas

18. Broken record

We are sometimes accused by children of nagging because we keep reminding them of the same things over and over again. When we want to reinforce a particular message sometimes it pays to do it in a different way. Try using affirmation posters around the classroom which remind children of key messages. Make them stand out by using a paper style and colour which you use only for this.

> If you can dream it you can do it.

> The person who never made a mistake never made anything.

> No one can do everything but everyone can do something.

> Every journey starts with the first step, so take the first step – now.

21 great ideas

19. Pay it forward

Sometimes it's best not to wait for a child to achieve a desired outcome before they get the reward, because in some cases you may wait for ever! If you happen to know that Darren is a keen angler (but he's also your biggest problem and thinks you've got it in for him), next time you're in town buy him a copy of 'Angler' magazine. Very discreetly, without a big fuss, give it to him, saying something like, '*I was in town, saw this and thought of you*'. Just watch the reaction. Try 'paying it forward' sometimes.

20. Ask me what I did

We all love to be given the chance to tell others when we have done something we're really proud of, and children are no different from anyone else. Keep a collection of badges in your drawer which say only, '*Ask me what I did*'. When a child does something that is remarkable (for them, given their particular aptitudes and abilities) they are allowed to wear the badge for half a day. Anyone who sees that child around the school during that time has to stop and ask them what they did. For the child who doesn't get much positive feedback from their parents, try giving the badge to them at home time.

21 great ideas

21. Hey stop! Wait a minute Mr Postman
Not many children receive handwritten letters these days so next time a child does something of note, write a letter to them by hand on school headed notepaper saying how pleased you are with them and post it first class on Friday. They should get it on Saturday morning and they'll be amazed! They'll keep that letter for ever. More important, it will have made a significant impact on their perception of you.

A self-evaluation checklist

	A	B	C
I demonstrate the characteristics of effective teachers			
Children enjoy being in my class			
I use positive reward and recognition systems			
I greet children when they enter the room			
I use children's names frequently and positively			
We have our own collective celebration rituals			
I'm an empathetic listener			
I use a range of strategies to foster a sense of belonging			
We sing every day			
I use music to enhance the learning experience			
I compliment children whenever possible			
I take a personal interest in my children			
Use of fantasy and mystery is a regular feature of my teaching repertoire			
Positive language is used by children and adults alike			

A – strength   **B – not sure**   **C – area for development**

Being the 'Great Teacher'

Background

'Children have never been very good at listening to their teachers – but they've always been very good at imitating them!'

James Baldwin

Background

Primary children are such fun but don't always understand what we are trying to teach them – just look at these biblical insights, taken from the writing of young children:

Christians have only one spouse – this is called monotony

Noah's wife was called Joan of Ark

The Egyptians were all drowned in the desert

The Jews were a proud people but throughout history they had trouble with the unsympathetic genitals

The epistles were the wives of the apostles

Solomon, one of David's sons, had 300 wives and 700 porcupines

The first commandment was when Eve told Adam to eat the apple

Lot's wife was a pillar of salt by day, but a ball of fire by night

Background

Our understanding of teaching and learning has changed dramatically during the last few years as we have gained greater knowledge of how children learn most effectively. Brain research is adding to that body of knowledge so rapidly that we need to be reflecting constantly on our practice in order to incorporate the most up-to-date approaches in our day-to-day teaching and learning activities in the classroom. Allied to that is the growing influence of approaches such as accelerated learning, which has gained great popularity in recent years thanks to the pioneering and inspirational work of people such as Alistair Smith.

What follows is an approach to teaching and learning in the primary classroom which draws heavily on these influences and on my own practice over many years, and which reflects the key principles of accelerated learning already mentioned.

Two-way expectations

I have often seen teachers start the year by setting out their own expectations of the children. I was particularly impressed when I visited Cranmer Primary School in Mitcham, Surrey to see that every teacher also has an initial discussion with the children about what *they expect from their teacher* during the coming year.

You may be surprised at some of the things children came up with, as indicated in the following two examples:

Class 3T

Mrs Thomas expects children to:

- Be kind, considerate and polite
- Always listen to the person who is talking
- Never distract others
- Not wander around the classroom
- Always put up their hands if they wish to speak

The children expect Mrs Thomas to:

- Be kind, considerate and polite
- Never shout at us
- Not blame children for incidents until all the facts are known
- Start every day with a smile!
- Understand the needs of the class
- Help us learn from our mistakes

Two-way expectations

Class 6J

Mrs Joyce expects children to:

· Be silent and not fidget while she talks
· Avoid laughing at others when they make a mistake
· Always do their best and put effort into everything
· Work quietly and not disturb others
· Avoid calling out or interrupting when others
  are speaking
· Respect others and their belongings
· Be kind and helpful to others
· Be honest and truthful
· See others' points of view
· Look after the classroom and keep it tidy

The children expect Mrs Joyce to:

· Treat us as individuals
· Be fair and not take sides
· Listen to our problems and try to help us
· Be kind and caring
· Explain the work carefully
· Be patient if we need things explained again
  and again
· Make our room a happy and fun place to be
· Be firm but always fair
· Mark our work quickly
· Be prepared for lessons and be on time

Effective planning

Planning can easily take over your life, so when planning remember these key points:

- The purpose of planning is for children's learning, not for OFSTED inspectors or the school's monitoring programme, so make your planning as brief as you can, using bullet points and abbreviations wherever possible. Avoid narrative
- When delivering new input make sure the lesson plan includes starting with something that will engage the interest of **all** the children
- Make sure your plans include opportunities for children to learn by seeing, hearing, doing, and by repetition
- Every time you plan ask yourself, *'Will children enjoy this activity?'*. If you think the answer may be, *'No'* then change it
- Make sure you build in opportunities for formative assessment
- Plan interesting and stimulating plenaries which ensure that lessons don't just 'tail off' at the end

Differentiation

What is differentiation and how can you ensure it? You can differentiate for children's various aptitudes and abilities in a number of ways, including:

- By **task**, where differing groups of children work on completely different tasks, though the subject matter itself may be the same
- By **activity**, where all the children are working on the same task but approach it through different activities
- By **outcome**, where children are given open-ended tasks and challenges which allow them to produce outcomes at levels which reflect their own abilities
- By **delivery**, where the teacher recognises that children who have a particular aptitude for this subject are quickly able to understand a new concept and so have the key information delivered to them *before* the rest of the class. They can then get on with their activities while the teacher explains to the rest of the children. This is a particularly powerful technique for more able pupils

We differentiate to ensure that all children are challenged at an appropriate level.

Delivering great lessons

'What we want to see
is the child in pursuit
of knowledge, not
knowledge in pursuit of
the child.'

George Bernard Shaw

Delivering great lessons – structure

Now that you've done great planning and you understand the importance of differentiation it's time to start actually teaching your children!

With the exception of 'maintenance' lessons where children are continuing work begun previously it is important that you provide an effective structure (see above) for your teaching that promotes learning.

Delivering great lessons – connecting activities

Teachers sometimes launch into new modules of work without first finding out what children already know. Whenever introducing a new module or a new series of lessons, give children the opportunity to demonstrate their knowledge (and what they would like to know) through a range of connecting activities. Try some of these:

- Feely bag – one feely bag containing a number of items relevant to the new learning; alternatively one feely bag per group of four or five children, with children taking turns at trying to guess the various contents

- Timed, paired review – children are given a time limit during which each of them has the chance to say to their partner all they know about the particular topic

- Paired discussion – prepare a list of statements (rather than questions) related to the topic. Give each child one statement and ask them to decide what their opinion of it is. They then have to share their opinions with three other children

Delivering great lessons – connecting activities

- Tell a story – children sit round in a circle of no more than five. Every child has to think of a sentence which demonstrates what they know about the subject matter but they must keep it to themselves. The first child says out loud the first word in their sentence. The next child in the circle has to say the second word (which will obviously not be the same word as the first child would have said because the second child is thinking of something different) and so on. The sentence has to make sense and has to be related to the subject. The activity stops when someone says a word which naturally ends the sentence. At this point children take turns in saying what their original sentence was

- Knowledge Snowball – children sit round in a circle of no more than five. Every child has to think of a sentence which demonstrates what they know about the subject matter. Then go round the circle, with each child saying their sentence

Delivering great lessons – connecting activities

- Tell someone else's story – in groups of four, children pair off and each child tells their partner everything they know about the subject. The listener then has to tell the rest of the group of four their partner's story

- Props and artefacts – children love having things to look at and feel. If appropriate, gather together a collection of things that will provoke curiosity, interest and discussion

- Puppets – children of all ages just love puppets. If you've never used puppets in the classroom, now's the time to start!

Delivering great lessons – starts

Cubby Broccoli (film director) was once asked why his 'Bond' movies always started in such a similar way, with masses of excitement, adventure and action. His reply was that if he had to keep the attention of an audience for two hours or more he had to hook them in the opening sequence, which would also contain lots of unanswered questions. The audience would have to watch the rest of the film to get the answers. The recipe obviously worked because those films have been the most successful in cinematographic history.

Although you're not making a film, the principle is the same. The start of the first lesson of a new module of work which may have to be sustained for three or four weeks needs to engage the interest and curiosity of *all* the children.

Delivering great lessons – starts

Bring your lessons to life by trying some of these starts (in some cases they last all day!):

- Music – either play a piece of music or teach the children a new song
- Being in character – ever tried dressing up and taking on the role of a character for the day, eg Victorian schoolmaster to kick off a topic on The Victorians, or one of the knaves from 'Alice in Wonderland' to kick off three weeks' work on fractions?
- DVD – play a clip from a DVD to create interest
- Role play – children love role play and drama so do use this technique sometimes
- Total immersion – where the whole class takes on roles assigned to them for the day, eg they all become evacuees as an introduction to 'Britain since the 1930s'

Delivering great lessons – starts

- Mystery – place cut-out footprints leading from the classroom door across the ceiling and through the fire exit as a starter for a piece of imaginative writing entitled 'The Visitor'. Think of other ways of sparking interest through mystery

- Field search – hide plastic dinosaur bones in the school field in advance. Show children today's newspaper headline (which you have created) stating how dinosaur bones have been discovered in your school field. This could launch your science work on healthy living by starting with healthy bones

Delivering great lessons – starts

Starting lessons in an interesting and multi-sensory way really engages the interest of all the children. Once you have launched your lesson, continue to give the key learning points in the same multi-sensory way by recognising children's different learner preferences and using stimuli in the form of:

Visual
Use things such as artefacts, objects, posters, puppets, mime, things that children can engage with by using their *eyes*.

Auditory
Use alliteration, tongue twisters, music, discussion/debate, paired talk activities, tapes of sounds and other stimuli which require the use of *ears*.

Kinaesthetic
Use role play, drama, movement, mime, feely bags, manipulation activities (objects, playdough, other classroom resources) and other opportunities for children to learn by *doing, touching, feeling and bodily involvement*.

Delivering great lessons – starts

The enemy of a young child's understanding is the talking teacher. This doesn't mean that teachers shouldn't talk but it does mean that your talking at the start of lessons should be:

- Brief and concise – use language that gets quickly to the point. Say what has to be said and no more

- Simple and unambiguous – children are often easily confused, so describe your learning intentions and give other instructions at this stage in a clear manner, using language that children can understand. When you have done that, display those learning intentions and instructions visually (and visibly) to remind children of what was said

- After starting the lesson, give children a discreet way of indicating whether or not they understand what they have to do. Try using a traffic light system where each child has a red, amber and green disc on their desk – they display the appropriate colour so you can see whether they fully understand, mostly understand or haven't a clue!

Delivering great lessons – starts

In summary, this part of your lesson will typically take between 10% and 20% of lesson time and should always contain 'What, When, How and Why' information.

What? Tell children exactly what they are going to do today and how it fits in both with what they have already learnt and what they will learn in the future.

When? Give children an indication of the breakdown of the lesson, telling them how much concentrated work time they have before a concentration break and how long each part of the lesson will be.

How? Explain clearly how today's work is to be completed and set out, and the nature of all tasks involved.

Why? Always explain to children why they are doing a particular piece of work. Children need to know the point of what they are doing and where it leads.

Display the what, when, how and why where all children can see it.

Delivering great lessons – middles

Once the lesson is underway and the children are ready to work, ask yourself the following questions of this part of the lesson, which would routinely constitute between 70% and 80% of total lesson time.

Are working groups organised appropriately for this particular activity? ☐

Are all the children working at a level which challenges them? ☐

Do all children have the resources and materials they need for the task? ☐

Are the activities more than just filling in worksheets? ☐

Does everyone understand what to do? ☐

Are the children finding the work interesting? ☐

Is everyone on task? ☐

If you answer no to any of these questions, think about how to change your plans or organisation for next time. Whatever you do, try to avoid giving children activities which require them just to read information and write down what they find out – and **never** give them learning activities which require copying from the board. These are the least effective ways of getting them to internalise the new information.

Delivering great lessons – concentration breaks

Primary aged children find it very difficult to concentrate for long on tasks which require high-level intellectual focus. All children, but especially boys, begin to fidget and become easily distracted when they have been concentrating for too long. In many lessons, or in the Foundation Stage, learning activities may naturally have movement and other breaks built in. Where this is not the case, try to build short concentration breaks into your lessons. You'll find the children return to their work much more ready to focus and concentrate.

The next few pages offer some ideas for concentration breaks. The list is certainly not comprehensive but it should at least give you a start. Try making up your own breaks and use the ingenuity of your children for more ideas.

There is no hard and fast rule about when to schedule concentration breaks – use your own experience and the knowledge of your children to decide, but in each case your break should last no longer than two or three minutes.

Delivering great lessons – concentration breaks

Discussion
Do your children talk too much? I'd be very surprised if you said no – it's completely natural for children to talk, but we keep telling them to stop talking and get on with their work! Build in talk activities in every lesson as part of the learning. That way, because children know there's a talk activity coming up they are much less likely to talk when they shouldn't. Try paired discussion as well as group activities. For example, if you've been teaching about rivers, give them the task of talking together to come up with five ways that rivers help us.

Timed challenge
Give the children one minute to complete a given task. For example, during a literacy lesson where they have been learning about words beginning with 'pl' give them one minute to come up with as many words as they can beginning with 'pl' or with 'pl' in the word. The winning pair/trio/group gets to read out their list of words to the class.

Delivering great lessons – concentration breaks

Reflecting/thinking activity
Use thinking activities to allow children to reflect. In an RE lesson where they have been learning about caring and sharing ask them to think about one occasion in the last week where **they** gave up **their** time to show caring or sharing to someone. After a short while give them the chance to tell a friend about it.

Brain Gym®
Brain Gym® activities were first devised to help activate both left and right sides of the brain at the same time. As well as that they're fun! Various examples can be found in *'Brain Gym'* by Paul and Gail Dennison, but for the moment, try the two overleaf which work well with all ages.

Delivering great lessons – concentration breaks

Loco - motion
1. Start with arms by sides.
2. You're a train; move your arms as if they are the wheels.
3. There's a problem with the train! One of the wheels is moving backwards!
4. Move one arm clockwise and the other anti-clockwise.

Make a fist of it
1. With both arms raised in the air, make fists. (Keep arms raised throughout.)
2. Left hand: raise thumb then fold away, raise little finger then fold away.
3. Repeat with right hand.
4. Repeat with both hands together. Easy so far?
5. Raise left thumb and right little finger together. Fold.
6. Raise right thumb and left little finger together. Fold.
7. Repeat stages 2 and 3 several times.

Delivering great lessons – concentration breaks

Number challenge

Most children love number challenges so use them, especially when the lesson *isn't* numeracy. For example, for a Year 3 class:

> If I gave half of our class (of 32 children) 16p each how much would it cost me? You can work in pairs but you can't use a calculator.

Word challenge

Word challenges can either be connected with the learning activity or be nothing to do with it. For example, if you have been learning about adjectives you can give the children the task of finding as many adjectives as they can to describe 'clown' – so, 'funny clown', 'happy clown', etc. This works well if you give them a time limit.

Delivering great lessons – concentration breaks

Physical breaks
These are best used when it has become obvious that children need physical movement because they have become restless and fidgety.

1. Ask all the children to stand up and find someone in the room who they don't normally work with. Using their finger they should draw a mathematical shape (square, circle, triangle etc) on their partner's back for them to guess. Then swap round. They can choose three different people to try this on.

2. Give each child a small soft object, such as a cloth ball. They have to throw the ball up no higher than head height and catch it. Before catching it they have to clap their hands together. Children who are good at this should clap their hands as many times as they can before catching it.

3. Children clap a rhythm, which you lead. Start with something easy, becoming harder as you go along.

4. Ask children to assign themselves a number between 1 and 5. Give them a simple sum (eg 9 - 5) and if the answer is their number they have to stand up, turn around and sit down again. Make sure you do enough for everyone to have a go.

Delivering great lessons – concentration breaks

Musical
Children love to sing, so put together your own repertoire of short fun songs you can use with your class. Try to choose songs which have humour and/or movement. Try this two/four part round:

Not only do children like to sing, they also like to listen to music. Sometimes you can take a break for two or three minutes (perhaps when they have been working really hard for a long period of time) when you just say, '*Let's relax for a few moments while we listen to this*'. Again, develop your own repertoire of music which you can use with your class. Try to ensure it is multi-cultural and represents a variety of musical styles.

Delivering great lessons – concentration breaks

Quiz
Quizzes work particularly well with all ages, but you'll need to determine what kind of quiz works best with your children. Try general knowledge to start you off and remember, the break need only last two or three minutes, so don't overdo the difficulty of the questions. Children can work alone, in pairs or in groups for this activity – you decide.

Logic puzzle
A fox and four chickens need to cross the river. There is a boat available which can carry no more than three at a time. The fox must not be left alone with one chicken at any time because he will eat it. How can they all get safely across? Work in pairs.
(Answer on page 126)

Delivering great lessons – plenaries

To ensure that children have understood the key learning points try to leave time at the end of every lesson to recap the learning. The point of the plenary is:

1. For children to internalise the key learning points so that they don't forget them.
2. For you to ascertain what has been well taught and learned and what has not been so well understood so that you can identify what you need to go over again next time.
3. For the lesson to finish on a high. Children tend to remember the last part of a lesson and that is often what they bring mind when they next have that subject or activity.

Once children reach this point in the lesson they know playtime/lunchtime is coming next. Their thoughts turn to who they will play with or what game they are going to play. So:

- Make sure your plenaries involve all children and are **fun, short and to the point**
- Avoid plenaries where you talk and they listen. Children remember more when they **say things out loud to someone else** than when they are passive

The lesson starts described earlier can be used as plenary activities, or see following.

Delivering great lessons – plenaries

> 'We learn to do something by doing it. There is no other way.'
> **John Holt**

Puppets
Puppets can be used at any age. Don't think your children are 'far too old for that sort of thing'. One child in a group holds and works the puppet. Every other child in the group takes turns telling the puppet one thing they have learned today, with the puppet holder answering each statement with a positive affirmation statement of their own. Try other ways of using puppets with your children – they are readily available in children's toy shops and in the major educational catalogues.

The three 'Rs' – rhyme, rhythm and rap
Get children in pairs to make up a short rhyme, rhythm or rap to contain the key learning points of the lesson. If there's time, give those who wish the chance to perform theirs to the rest of the class, or to start the next lesson with it.

Delivering great lessons – plenaries

Role play

Every child makes up one sentence which states what they think is the most important thing they have learned in today's lesson. Everyone gets up and has to go to three other children, one at a time, and say their sentence. But just to make it fun they have to say it:

- In the voice of Bugs Bunny, Mickey Mouse or their own favourite cartoon character
- In a whisper
- In a sympathetic way
- In an excited way
- In a deep voice
- Very quickly or very slowly
- In a 'posh' voice, which the listener then has to repeat back to them

Develop your own variations on the theme – children really enjoy this kind of activity!

Delivering great lessons – plenaries

Postman Pat (Year 2 to 6)
Each child is given a blank piece of paper and has to write on it what they think was the most important thing they learned today. Postman Pat (one child) collects all the papers, mixes them up and delivers them around the class. Children then have to try to find the owner of the statement given to them by approaching a child, reading out the statement and asking, *'Is this your statement?'* The listener has to answer honestly but without using the words, *'Yes'* or *'No'*, until all the writers are identified.

Quiz
In advance, prepare a multiple choice quiz with no more than five or six questions, each with four possible answers (include humorous possible answers as well as outrageously impossible answers) containing the key learning points of the lesson. Administer the quiz and award a small prize or reward to the winning individual, pair or group.

Alternatively, borrow the quiz format from TV programmes such as *'Millionaire'*, *'Weakest Link'* and others and use it for yourself.

Variety

Great teachers know when to vary their teaching style or use different organisational systems to best effect in the classroom, so try to vary your approach by:

- Experimenting with different furniture layouts to accommodate different subjects and activities – be prepared to move the furniture around to facilitate this
- Try different groupings of children such as all girls, all boys, home groups (where children choose who they work with) or away groups (where you choose who they work with)
- Sometimes working in silence, sometimes allowing discussion
- Developing different teaching styles, eg 'instructional', 'interactive', 'co-operative'
- Using open-ended as well as closed activities and tasks

Memory mapping

Your children cover a huge amount of content each week and they are expected to remember it all. However, how can they remember it if no-one teaches them how? Memory maps can be used in a variety of ways, sometimes to organise thoughts visually, as in the example below, and sometimes as an aid to memorising key information, as explained on pages 81 and 82.

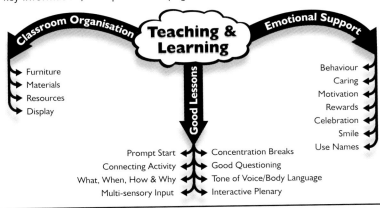

Memory mapping

1. First of all children will need to be taught how to construct a memory map. This will take time and you will need to work closely with them to teach them how to do it. Perhaps you could do this during your 'Learning to Learn Week' (see p100).

2. Memory maps need to be drawn individually by the children themselves because the information on the memory map needs to have come out of the child's head in the first place – **you** can't draw their map for them.

3. The memory map is drawn at the end of the module of work and is intended to be a visual representation of the key points learned during the module.

4. The memory map will contain a series of 'triggers', each of which will remind the child of an element of the work covered. The triggers will be visually memorable, perhaps using colours, shapes, symbols or something personal to the child. They will also remind the child of how they learned the information in the first place, perhaps using rhyme, rhythm, mnemonics or other memory tricks and techniques you have taught them.

Memory mapping

5. Once the memory map is drawn and you have checked it to make sure that all the relevant learning points are included, display it on the classroom wall near where the child sits and leave it there for a period of about a month. Give children regular opportunities to look at their maps, to share their map with a friend, or even give a short talk to their group about the content of the map. Children (being vain creatures anyway) will regularly look at their work while it's on the wall. The subliminal memorising that goes on in this way ensures that when the memory map comes down off the wall the children can still visualise it in detail, even though the map itself is gone. Whenever they need to remember the information learned in that module of work all they have to do is visualise the memory map and out comes the information.

Using memory mapping can be a powerful way of helping children to remember key information. It may work really well in your class but it is a technique that works much better if adopted by the whole school.

Tone of voice and body language

From a very young age children begin to be aware of tone of voice and body language. They very soon learn to pick up the signs from others that tell them of approval, disapproval, happiness, sadness and a thousand and one other emotions we all express at different times to children.

Think about your role in the classroom and the subtle signs you are giving the children all the time which are hidden away in your tone of voice and body language.

Going back to page 30 and the child's perception of you, if we really want children to feel we care about them as individuals, we must be aware of expressing that to them in everything we do every day – even when we have to reprimand them. Don't forget, we should be reprimanding the behaviour not the child.

Assessment and feedback

Formative assessment

Research evidence from people such as Shirley Clarke, Dylan Wiliam and Paul Black shows that the most effective means of helping children to progress is by using formative assessment and feedback techniques. Although there is a place for formal marking structures in your practice, try to ensure that your feedback to your children is:

* Mostly **verbal**
* ***Immediate and authentic*** – don't say work is *'fantastic'* if it's ordinary
* ***Educative*** and tells them exactly why it is good/not so good
* ***Specific*** and reflects what you asked them to do in the first place, so start lessons by identifying for the children exactly what it is you will be looking for
* ***Frequent*** – you will know which children require constant support and encouragement and which don't. This means you can't sit in the corner with a queue of children at your desk. Move around and intervene as necessary
* ***Without threat and sanction***
* ***Proactive*** – ask them to tell you what they think of their efforts before you tell them what you think: *'How do you think you could have improved this...?'* or *'What do you think are the best features of...?'*
* Make it an essential **part of the learning cycle**

Assessment and feedback

Marking

Although you may try to make most of your feedback verbal, some will inevitably be in the form of written marking. In those cases, wherever possible try to:

- Do the marking with the child at your side
- Make the comments meaningful and positive, so don't just write *'good'* or *'great'* – tell them exactly **why** it was good or great
- Identify lots of things the child has done well
- Keep negative comments to a minimum and where possible indicate how the work could have been improved
- Use language appropriate to the age and ability of the child
- Use the school's marking code and if the school doesn't have one, suggest to the head that you introduce one
- Don't spoil their work with your marking

Find out more about formative assessment by reading *'Inside The Black Box'* by Paul Black and Dylan Wiliam.

Questioning

You will find that when you ask questions of your children you often just get the same groups of hands going up. This is because some children:

- Don't think they will have anything worthwhile to contribute
- Think more slowly than others and can't get to their answer quickly enough, so by the time they finally get there they don't bother to put their hand up
- Feel embarrassed to contribute out loud in front of everyone
- Are worried about giving the wrong answer because of the put-down looks or comments they may get from their classmates
- Didn't understand exactly what you meant
- Feel intimidated by the way you ask your questions
- Would rather listen to others than make their own contribution

Questioning

In order to get more children involved, try changing your questioning technique so that instead of *asking* questions you *pose* questions.

For example instead of saying, *'Who can give me the names of three types of triangle?'* say, *'I'd like you to think about all the different types of triangles you know. Now turn to your partner and between you see if you can come up with three'*. Give them a couple of minutes to discuss this, ask them to decide who is going to be 'A' and who is going to be 'B' (or Frog/Toad or Slug/Snail, etc) then tell all the 'B' children to put their hands up. *You* then choose who gives you, not three, but one answer. I guarantee they'll all have an answer to give. This gives you the chance to include whichever child you feel needs to contribute.

You can use this same technique with groups, where the group discusses the possibilities but *you* allocate one child to be group spokesperson.

Experiment with different questioning strategies such as these, but always try to ensure that *all* children are involved, not just a few.

Gender

Have you ever wondered why it's mainly boys who get into trouble in school, or why it's mainly girls who are so good at literacy activities, especially reading? There isn't space in a book such as this to go into too much detail about issues of gender but it is important to consider some of the factors which may be contributing to the gender differences in attainment, achievement and behaviour in our schools.

- Primary schools are disproportionately staffed by females, in some cases 100% female staff. Although this in itself may not be a problem, it is likely that the school environment is very 'girl friendly' because we all tend to operate in a way which reflects our own gender identity

- Boys tend to learn in an active/competitive way, whereas girls tend to learn in a passive/co-operative way. Try to structure equal proportions of both kinds of learning activities when you plan your lessons. Use competitive language when setting up certain tasks, eg *'You've got five minutes to get all this work finished – bet you can't do it in that time'*

- Boys tend to prefer reading and writing activities that don't require lots of reading or 'narrative' style writing, whereas girls are happy with that. Again, try to provide opportunities for both kinds of work

Gender

- All children, but especially boys, have a limited concentration span, so be sure to incorporate movement in every lesson

- Girls tend to be unconditional and more self-motivated as learners – they will do whatever you ask **simply because you asked them to**. Boys need to know why they're doing things and what they get out of it, so tell them what, when, how and why – every lesson!

- Boys' sense of hearing is not as acute as girls' – make sure they are **always** looking at you when you give them instructions. Keep the number of instructions to a minimum and even ask them to repeat back the instructions to be sure they have understood

- The things that girls do naturally, such as working co-operatively or presenting their work neatly often leads to approval, reward, praise and recognition. However, the things that boys do naturally, such as being competitive, working alone, being highly active and needing danger, excitement and risk, often lead to disapproval and sanction. They don't always feel that they can express themselves fully

Take account of these factors when planning and teaching.

The good lesson

If you have incorporated all the various ideas so far into your teaching repertoire, you will be delivering exciting, stimulating learning opportunities for your children. In fact you will be delivering 'The Good Lesson' most of the time. Use this as a checklist for your own lessons.

Very well planned with appropriate differentiation ☐

Connected to the previous learning ☐

Start positively and crisply and are delivered enthusiastically ☐

Children told what, when, how and why, and this is displayed visually ☐

Explanation is focused and to the point ☐

All the learners are engaged by multi-sensory input ☐

Working groups are organised appropriately ☐

Voice and body language are used positively and effectively ☐

Children are reminded what, when, how and why ☐

Concentration periods and breaks are clearly defined ☐

Quality intervention and feedback are ongoing ☐

Learning is recapped and lessons end on a high ☐

Behaviour management

Many teachers make the mistake of thinking that classroom behaviour management is just about administering the school's behaviour policy and making sure there are plenty of rewards available in the classroom. It is certainly that, but much more besides. Children's behaviour should not be seen in isolation; it should be considered as part of a holistic approach to managing children as individuals and taking account of **all** their needs – as people first and as learners second. Children's behaviour is most likely to be good when:

- They feel their teacher and other adults like and care about them as individuals
- Learning is fun, based on what I have already talked about in this book
- There is a **positive and emotionally supportive** environment
- Parameters for behaviour are clear and unambiguous
- The behaviour management system is overwhelmingly based on positive reward and recognition rather than sanction
- Every child regularly 'feels' success and achievement
- There are no 'favourites' and no child ever feels victimised
- The teacher is always fair and consistent

Behaviour management

Once you have created the conditions for good behaviour to exist, you then need to be proactive in maintaining a culture in which every child wants to behave well. This hinges on the quality of the personal relationship *you* develop with every one of your children, but especially the most challenging children. In order to do this:

- Try to avoid being out of your class at all (on courses, etc) during the first half of the autumn term. Continuity is vital in establishing the culture that will exist for the rest of the year

- Pay into your children's 'emotional bank' by paying them compliments, noticing when they do the things you're looking for, praising them for it and speaking kindly to them. Do these things for all your children, but do them especially for your most challenging children. You will find that if the emotional bank is full it is much easier to deal with poor behaviour when it arises, because the child feels you do care about them. If the emotional bank is empty it is much less likely that the child will want to change their behaviour, because they feel you don't care about them anyway

Behaviour management

- When planning, put an inordinate amount of time into developing exciting and stimulating lessons during September
- Always find time to listen and talk to individual children when they need you, especially your difficult children. It's possible that you may be the only person who ever does find time for them
- Try not to reprimand children in front of their friends and try to avoid shouting at one child across the heads of the whole class during a lesson. If you really need to reprimand an individual, do it privately now or save it till later
- You may sometimes need to raise your voice but try *never* to shout
- Once you've developed strong personal relationships with your children you can use statements like, '*You've really let me down*' or, '*I am so upset about this*' or, '*I never thought you'd do anything like that*' because they will be more upset at letting you down than anything else. If you haven't developed strong relationships, these kinds of statements don't work

 '*You've really let me down*'

 '*I am so upset about this*'

 '*I never thought you'd do anything like that*'

Behaviour management

There will be many times during the course of a term when you will have to deal with conflict, sometimes between two children and sometimes between groups of children. Don't abdicate responsibility by passing it on to someone else; learn to deal with it yourself by having a few strategies up your sleeve which you can use if and when you need to.

Conflict avoidance

Rather than having to deal with conflict once it happens, it is far better to have strategies that help avoid conflict developing in the first place. This requires you to be proactive at all times and be on the lookout for possible conflict situations in the classroom. Many of the things we have already talked about in this book will help to create a classroom where conflict is rare, but in addition try to:

- Use circle time regularly to give children the chance to show how they feel
- Spot it coming – and intervene as early as possible. Identify the triggers that lead your most problematic children into conflict and nullify them. For example, if you know that Ahmed and Jack can't stand the sight of each other, there's no short-term advantage in having them work in close proximity at any time, even if in the long-term you will want to try to teach them both greater tolerance

Behaviour management

Conflict avoidance

- Listen attentively to grievances. Always give children the chance to tell you what is upsetting them, and respond to what they say affirmatively and supportively, without judgement. Give credit to their feelings
- Show you care – overtly by the things you say and the things you do
- Be polite at all times – children learn what they live
- See the funny side
- Plan brilliant multi-sensory lessons
- Involve the students in everything you/they do – frequently ask them what they think about particular lessons/subjects/activities
- **Never** use sarcasm
- **Never** reprimand in front of others
- **Never** use humiliation or embarrassment

Behaviour management

Conflict de-escalation
Sometimes, in spite of your best efforts, situations of conflict will arise, but it's still not too late to solve the problem before it gets out of hand. If a situation looks like it's escalating there are things you can do to de-escalate it:

- Don't take it personally. The worst thing to do is let your emotions get the better of you, so stay calm and as dispassionate as possible

- Don't stoke the fire and fan the flames! Listen more than you talk but if you do have to say something, make it positive and non judgemental. Speak using supportive, sympathetic and empathetic language and body language

- Keep control of yourself. If you lose control the situation will escalate

- Don't drag up previous misdemeanours – deal with this issue alone and don't use expressions like, *'Well what can I expect after last week's incident?'* or, *'I might have known you'd do something like this'*

Behaviour management

Conflict de-escalation
* Empathise – put yourself in the child's shoes and try to see it from their point of view
* Back off or back down. There is no shame in compromise
* Provide time out to prevent the situation getting worse
* Reprimand the behaviour not the person
* Be conciliatory and genuinely humble
* Don't get into an argument!
* *Always* give them a way out – give them the chance to make amends
* Avoid making it a challenge. If you use the kind of language that makes it seem like a challenge, then many children, boys especially, will rise to it and take you on

Behaviour management

Conflict resolution

Unfortunately, there will be occasions when nothing you do can prevent conflict occurring and by the time you are involved it's a case of sorting out a problem that has already taken place. If tempers are frayed and people are angry, now isn't the time to deal with it. Give both parties time and space to cool off before dealing with it, but don't leave them in the same space! Make sure you:

- Give both parties the opportunity to explain their side of the story, without interruption.
- Ask questions so that you have the **whole** story. Then repeat the story back to them to make sure you've got it right
- Don't take sides
- Don't allow yourself to become angry – you have to remain calm and dispassionate
- Don't become part of the problem by getting personally involved

Behaviour management

Conflict resolution

- Believe your children and everything they say, but don't assume that their story is accurate. They only have *their* perspective and few children are mature enough at this age to see it from anyone else's point of view. Try to get independent witnesses to verify the various statements made

- Be absolutely, unequivocally fair to both sides

- Involve both adversaries by asking **them** what they think should now happen to resolve the situation – you'll be surprised at how mature they can be when required

- Don't feel that there always has to be punishment meted out. Often it's enough to have sorted out the problem

- Return to the children involved a day later to see how things are then

Learning to learn week

The education process can sometimes be a real mystery to children because we don't always explain to them **why** we do the things we do. Try setting aside the first week of the academic year for a 'Learning to Learn' week, during which you don't cover any of your agreed curriculum. Instead, cover such things as:

- My expectations of you as learners, and your expectations of me as your teacher
- Our class ground rules for speaking and listening this year
- Hydration and why we need to drink more water
- Nutrition and exercise and why they are important
- The importance of sleep and how it helps us learn
- The conditions in which our brains are most effective for learning
- Memory techniques and tricks; memory mapping and how it can help us
- The structure of our lessons and why we need multi-sensory activities, concentration breaks and interactive plenaries
- Why we do homework

Include anything else you feel may be appropriate given the age, ability and particular characteristics of your class.

Setting homework

Whatever the reasons your school has for setting homework for children, consider the following points whenever you set homework activities. Make sure they:

- Reflect the level of interest and multi-sensory involvement you strive for in your lessons during the day
- Are varied and offer a range of different types of activity
- Are differentiated to accommodate children's aptitudes and abilities
- Are not mind-numbingly boring and repetitive
- Give children the chance to develop a range of different skills such as research, observation, thinking, collation of information, classification, reading, writing and calculation
- Don't require input from parents – this accentuates the problems of those children whose parents can't or won't help

A self-evaluation checklist

	A	B	C
We start the year with a 'Learning to Learn' week			
My planning focuses on children's learning and is brief and concise			
Learning is differentiated			
My lessons begin with a connecting activity			
I deliver the key learning points in a multi-sensory way			
I tell children what, when, how and why, then display it visually for all to see			
Concentration breaks are a regular feature of my teaching			
My lessons end with a plenary activity in which all children are involved			
I use a variety of teaching and organisational structures and strategies			
My tone of voice and body language are positive and supportive			
I use formative assessment			
Questioning involves all the children			
I take account of gender in my planning and teaching			
Behaviour is good			
Homework activities are interesting and stimulating			

A – strength   B – not sure   C – area for development

The Role of the
Primary Teacher

 Classroom
Organisation

 Creating the
Emotionally Supportive
Learning Environment

 Being the
'Great Teacher'

 Relationships

 Looking After
Yourself

 Successful OFSTED
Inspections

Relationships

Parents – occasional meetings

Parents love their children and need to know that you are taking good care of their offspring, so in all contact with parents make sure they are left with that perception. Parents may only meet you on a very few occasions in a whole school year; they are forming opinions about you based on the evidence they experience in these few meetings. You will usually be on home ground (ie your classroom) when a parent wants to see you, so bear in mind that if they've had the courage to come in and see you about something it's probably legitimate.

- If you have time to see them, greet them warmly with a smile then get to the point

- If you don't have time right now, apologise and agree a mutually convenient time later

- If a parent comes to you with a grievance, listen to them, believe everything they say and give them the opportunity to tell you everything about it. Don't dispute their view of things at this stage because their perception is their reality, even if you know they're wrong. If you can respond immediately, do so, calmly and unemotionally, explaining the facts clearly and concisely. If you can't respond immediately, promise you will investigate fully. Give them a day and time that you will get back to them and stick to it

Parents – formal consultation meetings

There will be occasions during the year when you will be required to meet formally with parents to report on their child's progress. You are likely to have a time limit for the meeting, so be well prepared on these occasions by:

- Being smart but not overdressed
- Making sure your classroom is tidy and well presented and that all work is marked and available for parents to see
- Keeping handy for reference, brief and concise notes on every child
- Keeping a watch or clock handy and sticking to time
- Starting the meeting by saying something positive about the child
- Keeping to the point and not getting drawn into long discussions
- Doing most of the talking to inform them of their child's progress. If parents want a longer meeting to discuss something specific, make a separate appointment
- Being sensitive to parents' feelings if you have to deliver bad news, and planning carefully how you are going to say it. No parent enjoys hearing bad news about their child!
- Keeping evidence handy to back up any statements you make about a child

Others

Other children
Your main responsibility is to the children in your own class but you will inevitably come across other children around the school, some of whom may one day be in your class and others of whom are brothers, sisters or friends of children in your class. So:

- Treat all children just as you would treat your own class
- If you see something going on around the school and you are the nearest adult, don't ignore it – what you don't challenge you condone, so intervene. All the children are everyone's responsibility!
- Have lunch with other children occasionally, even sitting with them in the school dinner hall sometimes

Governors
You will not have too much cause to meet with governors but when you do, welcome them with open arms, especially if they visit your classroom. And don't be nervous – they're probably as nervous about coming into your classroom as you are about receiving them. They're just ordinary people trying to support the school, so relax and treat them like you would any other visitor.

Others

Colleagues

Once you're in your classroom with your children you're on your own! But good teachers work closely with colleagues to ensure they are well supported in their wider role in the school. You need to try to get along with everyone else, so adopt some of the same principles you use in the classroom when dealing with colleagues.

- Greet colleagues with a smile – it's infectious

- Notice things colleagues do (such as taking an assembly, completing a display, dealing with a difficult child/parent, etc) and make a point of commenting on it, especially when it was the result of a lot of previous work, or if the situation was particularly problematic

- Help out if someone needs you – it could be *you* who needs *them* next time

- If you need support from a more experienced colleague don't be afraid to ask them – they won't know you need help unless you tell them

A self-evaluation checklist

	A	B	C
I am friendly towards parents and greet them by name			
Parents find me approachable			
During parent consultations I'm a good timekeeper and stick to the point			
During parent consultations I am sensitive to parents' feelings			
I get on well with other children around the school			
Children from other classes often come and find me to talk			
I welcome governors warmly into my classroom when they visit			
I get on well with the governors I have met			
I get on well with my colleagues			
My colleagues and I are mutually supportive of one another			
I don't fall out with others			

A – strength   **B – not sure**   **C – area for development**

Looking After Yourself

Staying fit and healthy

You don't need me to tell you that primary teaching can be an exhausting job, one which requires you to stay fit and healthy to do it effectively. In order to achieve this:

- Eat a proper breakfast and don't skip meals – keep an energy bar handy

- Eat more fruit and vegetables than you would think normal – you're exposed to a lot of illness and infection working with children, so you need to build up your resistance as much as you can

- Drink plenty of water during the day

- Make time for a lunch break where you have a complete break from the children, even if it's only for 15 minutes

- Get yourself fit by taking regular exercise and sticking to it, especially during term time. Commit yourself to this time and don't allow yourself to be deflected from it

- Make sure you get the amount of sleep you need

Managing stress

Teaching can be a stressful job, and while a little stress helps us all to function more effectively, problems can arise when stress begins to affect our ability to function normally. Avoid getting into that situation by trying to:

- Identify the things that cause you the greatest stress and systematically seeking help and support from colleagues to deal with these key stressors. Whatever you do don't just ignore them – *they won't go away*

- Set aside times in the week when you do your planning, your marking and other paperwork – and stick to it

- Aim to arrive early in the morning so that everything you need to do to prepare for your day is done at least ten minutes before the children arrive. That way you've got time to relax and think before you start teaching

- Put in place clear, well-understood systems and procedures for everything you and your children do

- Set aside certain times in the week (perhaps one particular day) when you do *NO* school work and find time for the things you like to do

Managing your professional development

When you start out in teaching you don't know exactly what the future may hold for you or where your skills and experience may eventually take you, so try to cover all eventualities by taking personal responsibility for your own development. Don't allow it to be left in the hands of someone else.

- Prioritise your key professional needs in the short-, medium- and long-term and decide exactly what you need to do so that they are met. Don't wait for your performance management meeting to discuss this with the school's Inset co-ordinator – do it NOW!

- It's difficult to take on a leadership position in a school without being able to demonstrate to those you lead that you know what you're talking about! If you think your future may lie in senior management, you will first want to be the best teacher you can be. Senior management will require great versatility and knowledge across the whole spectrum of primary education, so you should not restrict your professional development to one particular subject or area of expertise

Managing your professional development

- If you think your future may lie in one particular area or discipline such as science or special needs, then you will want to focus your professional development more on that and other related areas

- Although courses and conferences can be interesting and thought-provoking, don't assume that the best professional development comes from attendance at courses and conferences because it doesn't. If you really want to develop a new skill, go and watch someone you know to be pre-eminent in that particular activity in action. Talk to them about it then copy them. In time you'll develop your own way of doing things based on the expertise you 'borrowed' from them

- Create a file/folder divided into a number of different sections to contain all the relevant paperwork related to performance management, employment history, testimonial statements from employers, letters of commendation or thanks, cv, records of courses/conferences attended and so on. Keep everything filed efficiently for later use and reference

Managing your professional development

- From the moment you first start teaching begin to keep evidence of every worthwhile activity you ever do with your classes. Keep examples of work that children have done: photographic evidence of displays you have produced or things children have made in DT/science/art etc; video footage of class assemblies; drama/music productions or sports activities. Keep all this and more in a constantly updated portfolio, all annotated and chronologically organised for future use

- Keep up to date with what's happening in education by reading the TES every week and making time to read other relevant publications, magazines or books as needed

- Treat every opportunity that presents itself to you in your career as a once-in-a-lifetime chance and grab it with both hands. For example, you may be given the chance to lead a school visit for the whole Year Group to the Science Museum in London but you've never done it before. Say yes, you'd love to, then find out exactly what has to be done and do it – believe in yourself because you can't know if you'll ever get the chance to do it again

Managing your time

One of the biggest single problems affecting teachers is lack of time to do everything, but sometimes this is more to do with how you manage your time than the fact that there isn't enough time. So what can you do about it?

- Identify all the things that **must** be done on a regular, recurring basis and commit them to the diary, things like teaching time, staff meetings, aerobics workout, visiting Nan, etc

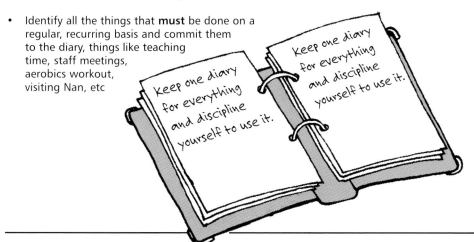

Keep one diary for everything and discipline yourself to use it.

Keep one diary for everything and discipline yourself to use it.

Managing your time

- Keep a running list handy at all times, on which you place everything that needs to be done, and don't try to commit things to memory. Once a week (I would suggest a Sunday evening, for half an hour or less) sit down with your list and your diary and move **everything** from your list into your diary, so that you start each week with a blank list. Once it is in your diary you must commit to honouring the entry

- Build in an appropriate amount of time **every** week (perhaps an hour) which is purely for professional reading

- Build in a 'blank' time (of about an hour or two) once a week in your diary which is there specifically to allow for 'slippage'. You will find that sometimes nothing comes in to fill the space and you can use it for whatever you wish

- If you can, go on a time management course

- Treat yourself regularly by leaving spaces in your diary which are purely for you!!

Managing the paperwork

You could easily drown in paper without good systems to manage this essential part of your work. You can keep on top of it by adopting a few key principles:

- Develop the skills of skimming and scanning and apply these rigorously to the various documents and papers you have to read. Most of your paperwork can be dealt with using these skills. Put all paperwork in three piles – for skimming, for reading, for recycling

- Identify which documents, books or publications **must** be fully understood and read these word for word

- Identify what paperwork is absolutely a waste of your time and bin it!

- Allocate time in your diary for dealing with the regular paperwork (see page 115 on time management)

A self-evaluation checklist

	A	B	C
My diet is healthy and balanced			
I always find time to have a break from the children at lunchtime			
I take regular exercise			
I'm fit			
I get plenty of sleep and sleep well			
I'm too stressed to be effective			
I take personal responsibility for my own professional development			
My professional development folder contains a full record of my achievements to date			
I am well-read			
Time management is a strength			
I keep on top of the paperwork			

A – strength **B – not sure** **C – area for development**

Successful
OFSTED
Inspections

Preparing for OFSTED

Whether you like it or not OFSTED will descend upon you at some point in your career. You can't avoid it so you might as well be circumspect about it and turn it to your best advantage. As a class teacher OFSTED will only be interested in you as a teacher and will be likely to observe you teaching once or twice during their visit. Don't get too worried about it – you know what you're doing so make sure they see you at your best.

- Once the date for the OFSTED is announced, look at your schemes of work and move things around so that during the visit you are teaching subjects and content with which you are most confident

- Don't go for safety – **be bold**! Work with year group colleagues to plan scintillating, exciting lessons which incorporate everything you believe is represented by good teaching and learning. Put an inordinate amount of time into your preparation so that your subject knowledge leaves nothing to chance if you happen to be observed

Preparing for OFSTED

- Sit in one of your children's chairs and look around at your classroom from their perspective. What does it look like, and more importantly what **should** it look like? You may not have much time to make changes to your classroom layout once OFSTED announce their visit, so make sure your classroom is organised for effective learning *at all times*

- Keep evidence of anything you're proud of which may **not still be visible** by the time of the visit to show inspectors when they arrive

- The night before the inspection begins enjoy a nice meal with nearest and dearest, or go out for the evening to take your mind off school

During the inspection

So, the inspectors arrive. The trouble is there's no guarantee that anyone will observe you teach, let alone that they'll see your best lessons, so be proactive. You've put time, effort and energy into this. Make it all worthwhile by:

- Getting up early on the first day and having a relaxed and unhurried breakfast
- Arriving early, getting everything ready well in time for the start of the day and then giving yourself fifteen minutes to relax, have a cup of tea, talk to colleagues, go into a cupboard and scream, or whatever else you need to do
- **Being proactive** and actually approaching the registered inspector on the first day and *requesting* that an inspector come and see your PE/literacy/maths lesson (you decide which one you really want observed) because you just know it's going to be brilliant
- Keeping your evenings free during the inspection so that you can relax. You will be feeling tense during this period so should find time to do what *you* want
- Trying to carry on as normal. Don't change your normal daily school routines. If you would eat lunch with the children on a Tuesday, do so this Tuesday; if you would normally have parent helpers hearing readers, then still have them

After the inspection

So, you survived! Was it as bad as you thought? Probably, yes. But it's all over now and you can go back to normal. When you receive the official report it will contain the findings of the inspection. Much of it may be of little interest to you, but there will be statements which refer specifically to teaching and learning and although you won't be mentioned in person you can quickly extrapolate from the general findings the parts which are applicable to you.

- If you were observed teaching, don't ignore the feedback you received from the inspector who observed you. Take it on board and endeavour to address the key points made

- Identify which parts of the report refer to the learning environment, quality of teaching and learning, behaviour and classroom management. Identify whether those comments apply in your case and see if there is anything you need to do to address the key issues raised

Useful references for primary teaching and learning

Good reads

Author	Title	Source	ISBN
Burgess, Ron	Laughing Lessons	Free Spirit	1 57542 075 9
Buzan, Tony	Master Your Memory	BBC	0 563 53728 0
Buzan, Tony	Mind Maps for Kids	Thorsons	0 00 715133 0
Buzan, Tony & Barry	The Mind Map Book	BBC	0 563 53733 7
Campbell, Don	The Mozart Effect for Children	Morrow	0 380 97782 6
Caviglioli, Oliver & Harris, Ian	Mapwise	Network	1 85539 059 0
Corrie, Catherine	Becoming Emotionally Intelligent	Network	1 85539 069 8
Dennison, Paul	Brain Gym	Edu Kinesthetics	0 942143 02 7
Faber & Mazlish	How to Talk so Kids will Listen and Listen so Kids will Talk	Avon	0 380 81196 0
Goleman, D	Emotional Intelligence	Bloomsbury	0 7475 2830 6
Gurian, Michael	Boys and Girls Learn Differently	Jossey-Bass	0 7879 6117 5
Hannaford, Carla	The Dominance Factor	Great Ocean	0 915556 31 6

Useful references for primary teaching and learning

Good reads

Author	Title	Source	ISBN
Hannaford, Carla	Smart Moves	Great Ocean	0 915556 27 8
Hoffman & Bartkowicz	The Learning Adventure	Learn to Learn	0 9535387 0 2
Hughes, Mike	Closing the Learning Gap	Network	1 85539 051 5
Jensen, Eric	The Learning Brain	Brain Store	0 9637832 2 x
Kagan, Dr Spencer	Silly Sports and Goofy Games	Kagan	1 879097 56 7
Loomans & Kolberg	The Laughing Classroom	Kramer	0 915811 44 8
Margulies, Nancy	Mapping Inner Space	Zephyr	1 56976 138 8
Neall, Lucinda	Bringing the Best Out in Boys	Hawthorn Press	1 903458 29 3
O'Brien, Dominic	Learn to Remember	Duncan Baird	1 900131 93 5
Smith, Alistair	The Brain's Behind It	Network	1 85539 083 3
Smith, Alistair & Call, Nicola	The Alps Approach (Resource Book)	Network	1 85539 078 7
Smith, Alistair & Call, Nicola	The Alps Approach	Network	1 85539 056 6

See also page 128 for titles in the Pocketbooks series

Useful references for primary teaching and learning

Good websites

www.alite.co.uk — Accelerated learning (Alite Ltd)
www.braingym.org — Brain gym (Brain Gym International)
www.mind-map.com — Mind mapping/memory mapping (Buzan Centres)
www.modellearning.com — Mapping (Model Learning Ltd)
www.nelig.com — Emotional literacy (National Emotional Literacy Group)
www.education.man.ac.uk — Formative assessment (University of Manchester)
www.p4c.net — Philosophy for children

Answer to puzzle on page 74:
Two chickens cross, leaving fox and 2 chickens behind.
One chicken returns to pick up remaining 2 chickens leaving fox on first bank and one chicken on the other.
Two chickens return to collect the fox.

About the author

Bruce Potts

Author Bruce Potts has extensive experience in infant, junior and primary schools over a period of 25 years. A former primary headteacher who has turned around both a failing inner city and a village school, he now mentors new headteachers, has led a variety of school/community projects as director of an EAZ and, as an independent education consultant and trainer, is widely known for his inspirational and motivational work in the fields of teaching & learning and leadership & management.

Bruce would be happy to help you develop any of the ideas mentioned in this book in your own school. He can be contacted through his website: www.primarytrans.com or directly by e-mail at bruce_bp@hotmail.com

Order Form

Your details

Name _____

Position _____

School _____

Address _____

_____

_____

Telephone _____

Fax _____

E-mail _____

VAT No. (EC only) _____

Your Order Ref _____

Please send me:

No. copies

Primary Teacher's _____ Pocketbook ☐

_____ Pocketbook ☐

_____ Pocketbook ☐

_____ Pocketbook ☐

_____ Pocketbook ☐

Order by Post

Teachers' Pocketbooks

Laurel House, Station Approach
Alresford, Hants. SO24 9JH UK

Order by Phone, Fax or Internet

Telephone: +44 (0)1962 735573
Facsimile: +44 (0)1962 733637
E-mail: sales@teacherspocketbooks.co.uk
Web: www.teacherspocketbooks.co.uk